Walking by Faith, Not by Sight: A Collection of True Stories

Nick Nichols

Published by Nick Nichols, 2023.

While every precaution has been taken in the preparation of this book, the publisher assumes no responsibility for errors or omissions, or for damages resulting from the use of the information contained herein.

WALKING BY FAITH, NOT BY SIGHT: A COLLECTION OF TRUE STORIES

First edition. June 15, 2023.

Copyright © 2023 Nick Nichols.

ISBN: 979-8223864080

Written by Nick Nichols.

Table of Contents

Chapter 1 | Not by Sight 1

Chapter 2 | Cucumber Mountain and Plumbing Parts 10

Chapter 3 | Granny Rides the Washing Machine! 15

Chapter 4 | God Going Before Us 21

Chapter 5 | Dizzy Salty Daughter 28

Chapter 6 | Three Teens and a Flat Tire 33

Chapter 7 | Picked by a Pickpocket 37

Chapter 8 | 5 Hp Outboard Witness 43

Chapter 9 | Little Boat, Big Boat, Big FREE Boat! 47

For Nick's Other Books | Simply go to: AuthorNick.com 56

I dedicate this book to the Lord Jesus Christ who makes all things new!...and who made my life profoundly new on February 2, 1971. Without Jesus, there would be absolutely no stories to tell.

~~~

"For God so loved the world that he gave his one and only Son, that whoever believes in him shall not perish but have eternal life." --John 3:16 (NIV)

~~~

I also dedicate this book to our adult children Holly, Heather, Christian, Brittany, and our three unborn children in heaven, Jonathan, Jessie, and Jordan.

~~~

Lastly, this book is dedicated to Barb, my lovely wife of forty-five years, without whom the reader would have a more difficult time understanding what I wrote. God knew best and married me to a live-in grammarian who rescued me from dangling participles, split infinitives, comma splices and the dreaded squinting modifiers!
~~~

Chapter 1
Not by Sight

<<>>

Sitting there at her sewing machine, my wife gave me her attention as I came into the room saying, "Well, I've got our road trip mapped out; it should only take three months, through three countries, and around 15,000 miles." She stopped sewing, looked at me with her loving, caring eyes, and sweetly said loudly, "Are you crazy! You can't be serious, we have three little children!" But I WAS serious.

In 1987 my wife had quit her teaching job at a business university to stay home with our young children; I had quit my job as an environmental scientist with a state agency to strike out on my own as an environmental consultant, so for the time being, we were both jobless. Now, with time on my hands, I wanted to come up to speed on some current environmental issues, so my plan was to fly to an environmental conference in Tennessee and then fly to Washington, D.C. to discuss some energy ideas with a friend who had helped design the COMSAT satellite system, and then fly home.

Another travel plan developed, however, when my wife said, "I'm not working, and you're not working, so why don't we drive the trip and turn it into a family vacation." So, sitting down with a map, I looked at driving from Columbus, Ohio, to Knoxville, Tennessee for the conference, and then realized we weren't far from Macon, Georgia, where I had some relatives, and that wasn't far from Sarasota, Florida, where some of our good friends lived, and that wasn't far from West Palm Beach on the other side of Florida where my wife had some relatives, and traveling up the East Coast, we had more friends and relatives right up to Boston.

And since I was on a roll at that point, the plan just kept rolling along from Boston to Chicago, down to Little Rock, Arkansas, to the bottom of Texas, down to Mexico City continuing to Guatemala City, up the West coast of Mexico, into Arizona, California, Oregon, Washington, up into British Columbia and across Canada, back into the States through Minnesota, Wisconsin, Illinois, Indiana, and finally........back to Columbus, Ohio!

That's why . . . when I presented my travel plans to my wife and at this point she clearly saw that she got a whole lot more than what she had originally bargained for, and so reacted with, "Are you crazy?" One good friend with great concern said, "Nick, I think you've gone off the deep end this time." My reaction was to go buy a twenty-year-old VW camper van!!

In the following weeks, we packed up the van with supplies for us and the kids and lots of spare parts and plenty of oil for the van. My son wasn't potty trained yet, so we had white disposable diapers stuck everywhere! Before leaving, a friend of ours gave us a little 3x3-inch plaque with a Scripture verse on it that read, "We walk by faith, not by sight." (2 Corinthians 5:7) We set the little plaque in a prominent place on our dashboard as it seemed the perfect motto for our trip.

The next day my wife, our five-year-old twin daughters, and two-year-old son climbed in the old van as I pulled the sliding side door shut. It was like boarding Noah's Ark only without the critters and the rain. Pulling left out of our middle-class suburban driveway, we worked our way to the interstate, and we were off!

I was enjoying the drive south out of flat Columbus, Ohio, the kids were playing in the back of the roomy camper van, my wife was sitting in the passenger seat reading her Bible and watching the rolling hills grow larger and greener with trees as we drove further south. The sky was a beautiful blue with wispy clouds, and all was serene as the old van purred along.

After passing through Kentucky into Tennessee, I noticed a lack of power as the van attempted to climb the hills. I chalked it up, however, to the van being a four cylinder that was loaded with family and supplies. But as we drove along, and as the hills got steeper, I became more concerned about the steady decline in engine power; then about half way up a very long high hill, it happened.

I felt the van jerk, and looking out the rear-view mirror, I saw a huge cloud of gray smoke coming out of the back of the van where the engine was located. I had flashbacks of a burning van I was in earlier in my life that caused me to have visions of flames and a possible explosion. I yelled to my wife to get in the back of the van with the kids and instructed her that when I slowed down, I wanted her and the kids to jump out the sliding side door. My intent was to get the van away from them in case it burst into flames or exploded.

In preparation for the exit, my wife pulled open the side door; then slowing way down, I yelled back to them, "JUMP!" Instantly, they all bailed out holding hands, tumbling into the tall grass by the road while I kept going till they were a safe distance away; then, I pulled the van to the side of the road, turned off the engine, yanked on the emergency brake, jumped out and ran back through the cloud of smoke to my family. We stood there and watched, but surprisingly, the big gray cloud drifted away, and nothing more seemed to be happening. Still, we waited.

After a good while, I walked back to the van, put my hand against the engine lid to see if something might still be smoldering on the inside, but the lid felt reasonably cool. Lifting the lid with great caution to inspect the engine, I feared that I might see all the wiring and parts burnt to a crisp like in my previous van, but to my complete surprise, they all looked fine, only covered with a layer of oil!

Checking the oil in the engine, there was not a drop on the dipstick, but since I had purchased plenty of oil before leaving Ohio, I was in good shape. After refilling the engine with oil, I cautiously tried to start the motor. To my surprise, it started! However, it was running very rough, like it was only running on three cylinders instead of four, and the smoke started blowing out of the exhaust pipe again. Going to the back of the van and putting my hand into the exhaust cloud, I felt it was oily smoke and not a fire-based smoke. Obviously, something had happened to one or more of the pistons, and oil was being blown out of the engine.

The van seemed drivable, so we all got back in, and slowly, very slowly, we continued climbing the long, high hill. Soon, we came to a filling station; we needed gas, and I needed to check the oil. While my wife and kids made a potty run, I started filling the tank with gas and noticed a small puddle of oil forming under the van and realized the engine problem was even more serious than I had originally thought. Praying, I said, "Lord, what do we do now? Is this the end of the trip? We really need your help! Thank you ... in the name of Jesus." As soon as I finished praying, my eyes were drawn to a white plastic audio cassette lying in the dirt in a nearby parking spot.

Letting go of the gas pump handle, I walked over and picked up the cassette. The side I picked up was blank, but when I turned it over, I saw that it was a music cassette by a Christian band I recognized. It was Petra's album, *Not of This World*, and again my eyes were drawn to the middle song called—"Not by Sight." I thought about the plaque from our friend that was sitting on our dashboard and was reminded that indeed we are to walk not by sight, but by faith! Right then and there, I decided that no matter how bad our situation "looked," we would go on in faith trusting the Lord.

Filling the van up with oil and with a full tank of gas, we headed back out to the road and continued coasting down hills, and climbing them at a snail's pace, all the time fogging the folks behind us with oil smoke. After about ten miles and a couple of stops to dump more oil in the van, the engine seemed to be getting more critical. It was starting to get dark as evening closed in, and I began to wonder what to do. In another mile or so, we saw a truck weigh station, and I decided to pull in. There were only a couple of guys working in the isolated station with no trucks around that needed weighing.

After going into the little building to inquire about a nearby auto repair shop, one of the guys said he had a friend that worked on VWs but more as a hobby rather than as a business, but he thought he might be able to help. He assured me that there were no auto repair shops nearby, and his friend was my best bet for getting the engine repaired. He called his mechanic friend, who suggested that we stay the night at a nearby state park, and then drive, if I could, to his place in the morning. He said he lived back in the woods, and we would never find his place in the dark.

He gave us directions to the park and his place and planned on seeing me the next day at 9 a.m.

We limped our way to the park, paid for a camping site, parked the van and got ready for bed by setting up the beds in the van, but before drifting off to sleep, we prayed and thanked the Lord for a safe place to stay and for a plan to get the van fixed. Waking early the next morning and figuring this was probably going to take more than one day to fix, I got out the only "tent" we had which was a screen house, set it up, and moved the family, sleeping bags, food, water, and cooking stuff into the screen house.

My family looked like they were in a cage for all to see as folks walking by on the nearby trail looked rather strangely at them. In my wife's own words, she recounts, "I remember feeling very silly; everybody knows you use a tent with sides to go camping, not a see-through screen house! What kind of novice campers were we?? Obviously, we hadn't taken Camping 101 or if we took it, we must have royally failed it!!! The passers-by had no idea we had a camper van that was in the shop being repaired."

This was back before the days of affordable cell phones, so as I drove off, there was no way for me to stay in contact with my wife or to let the mechanic know I was coming. Leaving early to make sure I had plenty of time to get to the mechanic's house, I followed his map through the narrow, secluded wooded park roads. It seemed like I was about half way there when the van died—it just quit. It was 8 a.m.; I got out my tools and tried working on the engine, cleaning oil off the connections and such to try to get it started again. By 9 a.m. I was hot and thirsty and realized I had left all the water with my family, and there was no other water in sight.

Hunting around in the van, I found a quart of apple sauce; figuring that it had liquid in it, I drank the whole jar which did little to quench my thirst. Back out on the engine, I needed to get it started to get to the mechanic. About twenty minutes later, I stood up from the engine and felt something funny happening inside of me! All of a sudden, I felt as if I had just drank a very large glass of cool water!! I thought, "Wow!" It took about twenty minutes for my body to break down the fiber in the apple sauce to liquid, and I felt completely refreshed and no longer thirsty! Loudly I said, "Thank you, Jesus!!"

A few minutes after that, I saw a large tractor coming toward me—it was the mechanic! He said he figured I may have broken down on the way, so he came looking for me. He hooked up my van, towed it to his house, and drug it up a very steep hill to his large garage. Even in perfect running order, my van never would have made it up his hill. In short order, he found the problem—a hole had been blown through a piston head! That explained the loss of power and the large gray oil cloud that traveled with us.

Our answer-to-prayer-mechanic said it would take him a few days to get parts and rebuild the engine, so we'd needed to stay at the park till he was finished. He drove me back to the park where we lived in our screen house for all to see for three days. I got pretty good at changing my clothes in a sleeping bag though my wife and family chose to take the long walk to the shower house. We literally came to understand what it meant to "live in a glass house." More than a cliché, it became our awkward reality.

After the van was fixed, our friendly and extremely helpful Tennessee mechanic picked me up and took me back to his place, and I drove our new happy, healthy, purring-like-a-kitten van back to my family.

It was the start of a new day and the beginning of our three-month, three-country, three-kid, 15,100-mile trip. We loaded up the van, piled in, pulled the ark door shut, and we were off . . . with a new engine and a renewed faith.

<<>>

"For we walk by faith, not by sight." —2 Corinthians 5:7 (KJV)

Postscript: Our trip covered all the places mentioned except we never made it to Guatemala because we were robbed on a subway train underneath Mexico City and banditos got my passport—but that's a story detailed in a later chapter.

[This story is dedicated to Karen and Denise DM. who met up with us in Boston during our long road trip. Karen also took the photo of our family aboard the USS Constitution at the top of the story. Thank you Karen and DD, you guys are awesome! —Nick]

Chapter 2
Cucumber Mountain and Plumbing Parts

<<>>

My friend yelled. Opening my eyes—I yelled! My friend yanked the steering wheel to put our truck back on the road barely missing a telephone pole. We'd left late in the evening from Columbus, Ohio, in a small truck packed with used clothes for a mission in Cucumber Mountain, West Virginia. After working a twelve-hour shift with no time to rest, it was 3 AM in the dark winding woods, and I'd fallen asleep at the wheel; my sleeping friend awoke just in the nick of time! We were shaken but thanked the Lord for keeping us safe!

Cucumber Mountain is a tiny hamlet buried in the bottom of the West Virginia mountains in McDowell County. At that time, McDowell County was the poorest county in the United States. Most of the coal mines had shut down and there was little industry in the area. Families that had been coal miners for several generations were now struggling on government support. It was an isolated area where one had to drive down into Virginia and back up into West Virginia to get to the mission.

We finally arrived and slept in the truck till morning when the old mountain missionary came and beat on our truck to wake us. With no introductions and straight to the point she ordered, "Take the clothes up to that small shed and pile them beside the other clothes on the racks, and then we'll have breakfast." She sold the used clothes to the local folks for ten cents or a quarter.

While eating breakfast, I asked her, "Why do you sell the clothes when the folks are so poor?"

"Well, I used to give the clothes away, but folks didn't take care of the clothes, and I'd see them lying in the yards or being used for rags, but I discovered if I sell the clothes to them, then the clothes become their property that they value, and they take care of them!" She smiled and shoveled another fork of corn mush in her mouth.

This old mountain missionary had been a gentle, single woman who had moved to these mountains and had been helping folks in the name of Jesus for the last thirty laborious years. Those years had turned her into a tough, no-nonsense-in-your-face, mountain woman with a great sense of humor who loved Jesus and the people she served.

On a later trip down to her mission, three of us brought another load of clothes. She decided to take the three of us for a ride in her old four-wheel-drive Land Rover back into a "hollow," an isolated section of the valley.

"I'm taking you boys to see a family I work with, and they just got electricity for the first time and are real proud of it! They're touchy about strangers, though, because of the amount of illegal 'moonshine' made in these mountains, so stay with me and don't go wandering off, or you might get shot!"

We learned later that there was no real law enforcement down there, and folks took care of things themselves. The week before, a man was caught with another man's wife and was chained to the back of a truck and drug around the mountains.

After driving over pitted mud roads and up a dry creek bed, we reach the house. The first thing we noticed was their electricity. They had one light bulb hanging from a wire over the front porch. Nothing else in the home was powered by electricity—only the porch light! While she visited with the family, my friends and I stood out in the dirt-covered yard by the car. Sitting on a pile of rocks, we saw two grimy little boys about five and eight years old. Both had big wads of chewing tobacco bulging from their left cheeks and were spitting "tobaccie juice" on the rocks.

I walked over and whispered in the older boy's ear, "You see my skinny friend over there; if you can spit some juice on his shoe, I'll give you a quarter!" With a grin, he went after my friend. Five minutes later after chasing my friend around the yard, I paid up—the kid was a good shot!

That evening back at the mission, after washing my hands in the brown and black mineral stained sink, I asked the old mountain missionary why there was hardly any water pressure and barely enough water to wash my hands.

She said, "The well is at the bottom of the mountain, so by the time it gets up here, there isn't much pressure. Years back, a group of Mennonite men stopped in and built me a water storage tank. The pump at the well would send a low volume of water up during the night and fill my storage tank; then all day long I had plenty of water and water pressure, but the plumbing went bad about six months ago, and what I have now is what I have—a trickle of water."

Having done some plumbing in the past, I asked her if I could look at the problem. Upon exposing the pipes, I saw the problem right off. It would take a one-half inch cast iron tee, a union, an end cap, two ninety-degree elbows, and two six-inch pipes threaded on each end. But we had a problem. The three of us would be leaving early the next morning back to Columbus, Ohio. The nearest town was War, and with the rugged roads, it would be impossible to get there before the hardware store closed. So, we were stuck.

But the old mountain missionary lady closed her eyes and prayed, "Lord! You brought a man here to fix my plumbing, and he needs some parts. Can you do something about that? Thank you!" She opened her eyes and smiled.

She said, "You know the little shed up the hill where you put them clothes you brought? Well, years ago, a lady stopped by and made me some nice sturdy clothes racks out of plumbing parts. Go up and see if there is anything you can use."

I climbed up the hill, entered the shed, pulled back the tightly packed clothes on the rack and stared dumb-founded. At the foot of the half-inch cast iron pipe clothes rack was a tee, a union, an end cap, two ninety-degree elbows, and two six-inch short pipes threaded on each end!

I disassembled the clothes rack for the parts and a few hours later, this faithful old mountain missionary was thrilled because her water was working again. And through her simple prayer, my friends and I were blessed and humbled by the no-nonsense-in-your-face love of God.

"Listen, my dear brothers: Has not God chosen those who are poor in the eyes of the world to be rich in faith and to inherit the kingdom he promised those who love him?" —James 2:5 (NIV)

Chapter 3
Granny Rides the Washing Machine!

<<>>

My 91-year-old grandmother on my mother's side was considered by all who knew her a "Prayer Warrior." Whenever this thin, frail woman would pray, I would always have tears come to my eyes! No matter what I did, I couldn't hold them back; she was so connected to the Lord. But at 91, Granny's mind was starting to slip around a bit. Not a lot, but enough to be noticeable.

One day when I got home from school, I found my mother sitting in the living room. Speaking of her mother, she just kept shaking her head saying, "Poor Mom, poor Mom!" She was kind of upset and laughing at the same time.

She told me that earlier that day Granny had decided to do her laundry. With great effort hauling her clothes down the basement steps, bump by bump, she drug them over to the washing machine. Slowly piling her clothes in, she dumped in the soap and hit start. She sat down beside the machine to wait since it was easier to do that than climb back up the steps.

Granny sat in Grandpa's creaky old black chair he used to sit in before he died and started singing hymns as she often did. Finally, the wash cycle was done, and the machine entered the spin cycle. That's when it started—THUMP, THUMP, THUMP—the rhythmic thumping turned into a BANG, BANG, BANGING sound! Something was off-centre with her clothes in the old washer, and all the vibration was causing it to bounce around on the bare concrete floor.

This was frightful to Granny! Somehow, she managed to fling her 89-pound frail body up and across the top of the washing machine trying to hold down the bucking bull! And doing what Granny did best, she cried out, "Oh Lord! Stop my washing machine and help me get my clothes washed! In the name of JESUS, Amen!!"

At that very moment, my mom stepped in the back door of Granny's house just in time to hear all the banging downstairs and Granny calling out to Jesus! She scrambled down the stairs to see Granny riding the washing machine!! She ran over and hit the OFF button and set rattled Granny back into her creaky chair. My mom started shaking her head and Granny started in to a "Praise Jesus" session for delivering her within minutes of her prayer!

My mom straightened her clothes around, so the washer was balanced and stayed with Granny till her clothes were done. Now sitting at home shaking her head saying, "Poor mom, she couldn't even think to just turn off the washing machine when it started banging around." But I, sat there listening in wonder!!

"Mom!" I said, "You got off early from work, something that almost never happens. You told me you were going to the store but at the last minute decided to stop by and see your mother. You arrived at the exact moment Granny was calling out to Jesus. And you stayed and washed her clothes. Her prayer to stop the machine and get her clothes washed was answered!"

My mom and I sat there staring at each other; we had just learned a powerful lesson from Granny. No matter what—PRAY!

<<>>

"Do not be anxious about anything, but in everything, by prayer and petition, with thanksgiving, present your requests to God. And the peace of God, which transcends all understanding, will guard your hearts and your minds in Christ Jesus." —Philippians 4:6,7 (NIV)

Postscript: Speaking of prayer, even now at age sixty-five I can still vividly remember as a very small child Grandma holding me in her lap while rocking me to sleep in her old wood rocker singing, "What a Friend We Have in Jesus."

Joseph Scriven wrote the song in 1855.

As a young man in Ireland life looked bright and promising. Having recently graduated from the university he was to marry and the day before the wedding his fiancé fell from her startled horse while crossing a bridge, as Joseph stood waiting on the other side, knocked unconscious she drowned in the river Bann. Joseph got to her as they were pulling her lifeless body from the river.

So very devastated by this event he deeply sought the Lord in prayer to cope with his pain. Wanting to leave the memories behind and start over he moved to the small village of Fort Hope, Ontario, Canada. There he committed himself to be the light of Jesus in the community and as a handy man helping only the people that could not afford to pay him.

Years later he fell in love again and before they were married his second fiancé died from pneumonia. His words were written in the fiery furnace of life. Now you know a little about the man behind the poem.

Speaking from his heart he penned...

What a friend we have in Jesus,

All our sins and griefs to bear!

What a privilege to carry

Everything to God in prayer!

O what peace we often forfeit,

O what needless pain we bear,

All because we do not carry

Everything to God in prayer.

Have we trials and temptations?

Is there trouble anywhere?

We should never be discouraged

Take it to the Lord in prayer!

Can we find a friend so faithful,

Who will all our sorrows share?

Jesus knows our every weakness

Take it to the Lord in prayer!

Are we weak and heavy laden,

Cumbered with a load of care?

Precious Saviour, still our refuge

Take it to the Lord in prayer.

Do thy friends despise, forsake thee?

Take it to the Lord in prayer!

In His arms He'll take and shield thee

Thou wilt find a solace there.

Joseph M. Scriven, 1855

Grandma who had a difficult childhood and lived through the Great Depression with six children and a disabled husband related deeply to this song. My grandmother not only loved the song, and believed the song, she also lived the song.

Chapter 4
God Going Before Us

<<>>

After arriving at the Fort Lauderdale Airport in Florida where my wife, our youngest daughter, and I were going to catch our flight to Costa Rica, we were greeted by our airline customer service agent who asked us our flight number and then redirected us to another line where we stood with about a hundred other folks staring at each other wondering what was going on. There we heard the rumors about our flight being canceled due to the start of a pilot strike.

That flight was to take us to San Jose in Costa Rica, our church missions team meeting point, before being taken to our final destination in the village of Rio Cuarto near Nicaragua. Knowing that we were on a schedule to meet the rest of our team, I said to my wife, "I wonder how the Lord is going to solve this problem?" We stood in line and watched as folks started arguing at the ticket counter about their canceled flights.

While waiting our turn, I thought to myself about the time years back when my wife and I with our five-year-old twins and two-year-old son boarded a tightly packed subway train under Mexico City. We wanted to take the kids to an animal park petting zoo we had heard about. What we hadn't heard about was that we would be passing through the notoriously worst area for pickpockets in all of Mexico! (To be safe while traveling in Mexico, I had purchased a Harley Davidson wallet that zipped shut and was on a chain connected to my belt.) We squished our way onto the subway.

I held the hands of our girls while my wife held our son with one hand and with her other hand hung onto my belt, so we wouldn't get separated in the dense crowd. The whirring whine of the electric engines started up and the subway took off, and all was calm for a few minutes. Suddenly, I hear my wife yelling, "NO, NO!!!" Thinking someone is grabbing my wife, I turned around to grab whoever was grabbing her.

Turning, I saw the chain attached to my wallet pulled taunt straight out into the crowd! In an instant, I see my wife grab the chain, give it a yank, and rip it right out of the pickpocket's hands. He had it timed so the subway train would be stopping in time for his escape—I saw him jump out the door and thought about going after him—then thought that would be stupid with me ending up lost from my family in a city of over 100 million.

We quickly checked my wallet, and the contents were safely zipped inside. However, we soon discovered another pickpocket had gotten my passport that was in my front left pocket!! We got off the subway and surfaced, knowing we needed to get to the embassy to report the theft. Standing on the corner near the subway entrance, we had no idea where we were or where the embassy was, and we spoke little Spanish.

I prayed, "Lord, we are in a serious jam and need some help. Amen!" Moments later, we hear someone in perfect English behind us ask if we needed help!! We turned around and saw this smiling couple. We explained our situation and immediately they hailed a taxi for us to get to the embassy, negotiated with the driver in Spanish on a price, and told us not to give him a penny more!

The taxi driver was driving an old VW Beetle with the front passenger seat removed for easy access to the back seat. When the taxi driver stepped out to open the door, I saw that he only had one eye!! Well, that could present a serious problem because with only one eye, you can't judge distance very well, and he was about to drive us through crazy congested traffic!! I held my breath and got in. He had some close calls but to our complete amazement didn't hit another car all the way to the embassy. I was impressed!

After getting to the embassy, we found out that getting the travel papers we needed in Mexico City were very expensive because of the bribes necessary to expedite the process. While wondering what to do, we bumped into a guy named Jose, who was anxious to practice his English with the Americans. After filling him in about our situation, he recommended that it would be easier and cheaper if we got our new travel papers in Oaxaca since we were headed there anyway. However, traveling to Oaxaca, which was over 300 miles from Mexico City, without any travel papers was very risky. Jose instructed me, "If the military pulls you over and takes you into their office, speak English very rapidly, use the word 'attorney' several times while you're talking, lay a big pile of pesos on the table, walk out, and don't look back!" Gee, that made me feel good about the trip to Oaxaca!

Praise the Lord, we made it into Oaxaca without being stopped. After asking a bunch of folks including police officers for directions through hand gestures and a few Spanish words, we found the "Embassy" after climbing up a dirty, dark, narrow hallway of stairs above a copy shop! I walked up to the lady at the desk, who very quickly became frustrated with my English because it was obvious to me that she knew absolutely no English!

I then tried the best I could to explain our predicament in Spanish as I frantically used my well-worn Spanish-English dictionary. As her frustration furiously escalated, I saw that we had hit a wall and were at a dead end. It was then I prayed, "Boy, Lord, I'm in deep crap now; we need some serious help here!" Out of the blue, once again, in perfect English from behind us, a man says, "Hi, can I help you folks?"

He was a Wycliffe translator who had just stopped in the embassy for a minute to pick up a document he needed in order for him and his family to fly out of the country later that afternoon. He had been waiting for months for the documents to be approved and he had just gotten the call that they were ready and arrived at the same moment we needed the help! He spoke to her in perfect Spanish and got everything straightened out for us, and we quickly and cheaply got our travel papers.

How thankful we were to the Lord for his timely intervention! While chatting with our new-found friend, he told us he and his family were flying out late afternoon but wanted to know if we would like to join them for lunch before they left. We gladly accepted, and he called his wife to let her know we were coming. He then gave us directions to his house since he had another errand to run before heading home.

There was all kind of road construction going on—it looked like a war zone. Parts of roads were missing, new sections were being laid down in other areas, detour signs were all over the place, and heavy equipment littered the landscape—so much so that I had to edge my van around them carefully. After we made the first few turns, we were completely lost!! It didn't take us long to realize that there was no way we were going to be able to find their house and were bummed that we wouldn't be meeting our translator's family and have the opportunity to thank him again for his help. "HONK, HONK, HOOOOOONK!!"

An old green Buick throwing up a dust cloud from the construction starts pulling up beside us while I'm driving, and in my side mirror, I see some lady waving her hand at us through her open window. When she gets right next to us, she yells through my wife's window, "Are you the folks from Ohio my husband invited to lunch?" I'm stunned! Surprised, we nodded, "YES." She yelled, "Follow me!" We followed the green dust-storm all the way to her home. She was on her way back from a store to get food for lunch and had spotted us! The Lord had rescued us again!!

Returning from my reminiscing . . . back at the airport in Fort Lauderdale, we finally made it up to the ticket counter four hours later! The airline gave us food vouchers for three meals, a voucher for an overnight stay at a nice hotel with a continental breakfast, a voucher for a taxi to take us to the Miami airport, and American Airline tickets for us to fly to Costa Rica the next day.

We had been very fortunate because later I found out that so many flights had been canceled due to the pilots' strike that the airline had changed their procedure and started only giving folks their money back and a $100 airline voucher.

The next day when we got to the Miami Airport, we discovered the airline had NOT booked a flight for us with American Airlines but had only paid for our flight! We were surprised when the ticket agent said, "We can get the three of you on the last flight, but you won't be able to sit together." I was curious as to why. She then volunteered, "Because there are only three seats left!" My wife and daughter and I looked at each other and were not surprised that the Lord had gone before us once again! . . . as He had done so many times before.

<<>>

"The LORD your God, who is going before you, will fight for you, as he did for you in Egypt, before your very eyes,"—Deuteronomy 1:30 (NIV)

Chapter 5
Dizzy Salty Daughter

<<>>

Passing by my youngest daughter, Brittany, lying on the couch, I said, "You look funny. I mean not funny, funny, as in Ha, Ha, clown funny, but the yucky funny kind of funny."

With her eyes closed she said, "Poppy!!"

"Ok," I said, "So what's wrong?"

Holding her stomach and with a grimace she said, "I'm dizzy and can't stand up."

I responded, "You mean you can't stand up as in vertical, upright, perpendicular to the floor, 180-degrees straight up, stand up kind of standing up?"

"Poppyyyyyyyy STOP!! I'm really sick!"

"Ok, ok," I said, and that was the beginning of many months of my dizzy daughter's dizzy spells.

At first, we thought it might be the flu or cold kind of thing because she also felt sick to her stomach, and it's always so easy to think it's just the latest thing that's "going around," but as the weeks followed, the periodic dizzy spells continued. A trip to the doctor couldn't find anything wrong, so he suggested we keep an eye on her to see if anything else developed.

Sometimes she would go for days without a problem, and then some days the dizzy spells were so bad it was impossible for her to attend school—it's hard to go to school when you can't even stand up!

After missing an excessive number of days of school, back to the doctor she went, but the doctor still had no explanation and, unfortunately, no remedy. This went on for about a full year when finally, much to our relief, we found a doctor that figured out the problem—Brittany had the dizzy symptoms of Meniere's (pronounced "men-yairs") disease a problem with the inner ear that causes severe dizziness. The doctor gave her a prescription, but our hopes that the medication would be the solution were dashed when it ended up making her even sicker!

During this whole ordeal, my wife and I had been praying and asking the Lord Jesus for wisdom about what to do or to outright heal Brittany. Now that she was having a problem with the medication, our prayers intensified! We were thankful Brittany made it through the school year, and we were so grateful for the patience and understanding of her teachers throughout the months of her unavoidable absences, but questions raced through our minds—questions like, "How long can this go on?" "What about the next school year?"

While these unspoken questions caused us concern, summer was just around the corner, and we had an opportunity to go to Nicaragua as a family on a missions trip to help build a church—but what about Brittany? "Should we take her?" "Should we cancel altogether?" After praying, we decided to move forward and trust the Lord for Brittany's condition and go ahead with our original plans to go to Nicaragua.

On the flight down to Nicaragua, I ended up sitting next to a medical doctor. He was a nice guy and a bit chatty and was headed to a medical conference in Managua, the capital city of Nicaragua, where he would be speaking. During the flight, he pulled out his laptop and started looking at a PowerPoint presentation, which was about healthy and diseased tissue in the human body. I explained that I was a biologist and asked if he would mind if I read his PowerPoint as he reviewed it.

He answered, "Sure . . . only this is an old computer and the battery may die at any time."

I said, "No problem," and thanked him for letting me read along.

The first presentation he was reviewing was fairly long, but one I found rather interesting. Then he fired up his next PowerPoint, and my mouth dropped open in disbelief. It was titled, "Meniere's Disease"!! EXACTLY what Brittany had! With rapt attention, I carefully read every slide.

The presentation went through the history of Meniere's disease, the symptoms and causes. Then his slideshow started covering treatments, including a list of medications that had proven helpful as well as a list of side effects that might occur. If that approach was unsuccessful for the patient, then surgery was the next step. A series of slides followed that described the various surgical procedures.

The next slide seemed to be added as an afterthought and was labeled "Nonconventional Approaches." Under the title the word SALT jumped out at me. The slide stated that because Meniere's was caused by swelling in the inner ear, some patients may find relief from a reduced salt diet. However, there had been no clinical testing to prove this approach. I thought to myself after reading that, "I wonder if daughter Brittany has been a bit on the salty side?"

The moment I finished reading the part about the salt, his screen went blank—as his computer battery died. Shaking my head, I mumbled in my heart, "Thank you, Jesus; I'm certain this was from you!!" I discussed it briefly with the doctor as the plane began to land. During our time in Nicaragua, Brittany didn't salt any of her food and didn't have any dizzy spells during the whole trip!

That was over twelve years ago, and Brittany is no longer our dizzy salty daughter!

<<>>

"Some trust in chariots and some in horses, but we trust in the Name of the LORD our God." —Psalm 20:7 (NIV)

Chapter 6
Three Teens and a Flat Tire

<<>>

Three months earlier we had moved to the island of Penang just off the Malaysian coast and south of Thailand. I was finally settling into my two-year contract teaching high school science at an international school, and my wife and I decided to visit the nearby much-acclaimed Butterfly Farm. They had 120 different species of butterflies flitting about sporting an incredible rainbow of colors. There were thousands of them flying all around us in their enclosed world of tropical flowers and nectar.

After completing our visit there, we decided to continue on the road that loops around the island and find the Tropical Fruit Farm. It will help to understand what traffic is like in Penang. Cars going every which direction, and at the same time, there are hundreds of motorbikes also going every which direction. Like a relative of ours who's lived here for a number of years said, "In Penang, road lines and traffic lights are merely suggestions." Traveling is a life-and-death endeavor; I was recently told that so many folks are killed on motorbikes that the police no longer keep track of the statistics. Even the Malays that live here admit that traffic is bad!

So, we were very surprised when our GPS routed us up to a very nice four-lane highway that was nearly empty! Following the road up into the mountain, we only saw a couple of motorbikes and a few cars go by. Traveling further up into the mountain, we decided our GPS was giving us false directions with the mountain coming between our GPS and the satellite signal. Turning back started to seem like a wise idea. We found a flat rocky area to turn around and headed back down the mountain in our very small, three cylinder, Malaysian car.

Minutes later the car started bumping along, and my wife who was driving said, "Is the road rougher than it appears or do we have a flat?" That was about the time I smelled the rubber. She pulled over, I got out, and our front left tire was flat as a pancake! While I was looking at the tire, three teenagers pulled up on their motorbikes and wanted to know if we needed help. I assured them we were good, and it would only take me a few minutes to change the tire. Besides, I didn't know if they were there to hustle us, rob us, or whatever. I kept trying to get them to move on, but they just stayed ... kinda laughing while they spoke to each other in Bahasa, the Malay language, and very broken English. Still, I persisted in politely trying to get them to l-e-a-v-e! Still smiling, they wouldn't budge.

Then I started thinking, "Lord, is there some reason these guys need to be here?" As soon as the prayer left my head, I discovered we didn't have a jack or lug wrench! When we were buying the car a month before, I checked the spare, jack, and lug wrench—all were good. Apparently, before we brought the car home, someone removed the jack and lug wrench!! We had no AAA membership there and mechanic shops are tucked away among hundreds of other little shops. But the one big teen kept repeating to us in broken English, "You rtree no gd, I cld mhs frnnd, h ees say gud muh ka n tik!!" Smiling we said, "What was that you said?" Straining to understand after a couple more smiles and repeats, we got it—"Your tire is no good. I called my friend; he's a good mechanic!"

Soon after, down the mountain below us we heard a revving motor and then saw a small sedan flying around the corner, swing past us at full speed, hit its brakes, slide sideways, peeling rubber with gray-white smoke billowing everywhere. The sedan makes the turn, aims at us, and then slams on its brakes right beside us, and out steps our smiling mechanic. He pulled off the tire, and the inside sidewall had a hole the size of my fist. I paid him, and gave the three teenage boys some money for their help, and all was said and done in less than thirty minutes!! Talk about speedy roadside service!

On the way back down the mountain, I prayed, "Lord! Thank you for helping us once again! Even when I didn't think we needed help, You knew we did and had those boys stay. And thank you that we weren't in regular Penang traffic and didn't have a wreck when the front tire blew a hole the size of my fist. Thank you Lord, our trust and confidence is in You, and You alone. Amen from Penang."

"... I have had God's help to this very day, and so I stand here and testify to small and great alike ..." —Acts 26:22 (NIV)

Chapter 7
Picked by a Pickpocket

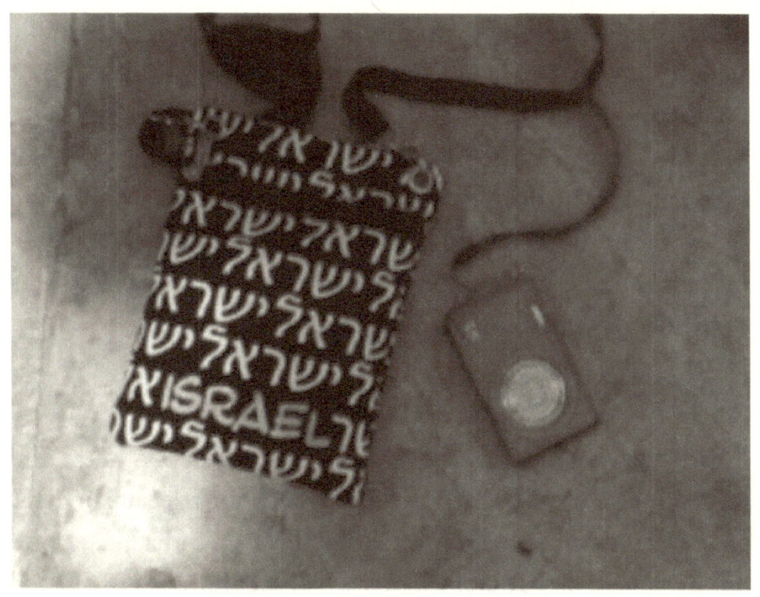

<<>>

Turning to my wife as I heard her panicked cry, I saw the sad, sick look on her face. We were standing just outside the Garden Tomb in Jerusalem on a street packed with people and vendors. I watched her frantically checking every pocket obsessively when she said in a deeply despairing voice, "My camera's gone!"

Instantly, we both thought the same thing—all our pictures of our trip around Israel. Gone. All our pictures with the new friends we had made. Gone. Over 3,000 pictures and videos. Gone.

That is…..until God intervened.

Our first twelve days in Israel were spent with the Joel Rosenberg tour—a truly heart-stirring tour of holy and historically significant sites all around Israel, giving us a new dimension of understanding to the Bible we had been reading for years. Plus, an added benefit was being blessed by friendships that formed, especially among our Bus #4 traveling mates! After the tour, we stayed on in the Old City of Jerusalem for another fifteen days to spend more time digesting what we had just experienced. This particular day put us on the street by the Garden Tomb.

My wife Barb, picks up the narrative…

I had been warned it was pickpocket territory. I knew the rules—hold bags close to your body and don't let anyone get close to you! Still, I became a victim. Nicky and I had just come out of the Garden Tomb, where we had spent hours just sitting, reflecting, and worshiping Jesus and the marvel of His resurrection. As I exited the gift shop, I read the sign warning about the thieves that hang out at the end of the walkway. I took notice and checked to make sure everything was "secure."

Once we reached that section of the road, I saw that the entire street had turned into a marketplace with canopied stalls selling everything under the sun. People were coming and going, and as we were walking through the packed maze of people, a man selling postcards approached us; I interacted with him a bit, but we finally let him know we were not interested. He refused to accept "No" for an answer as he trailed my steps. I ignored his persistence as I snapped a few shots of a cross on a historically old church that was just behind the vendor stalls.

With one last shot, I returned my camera to my pocket and rushed to catch up to my husband, but my effort to keep moving down the street and away from the postcard guy was suddenly blocked when a van that was trying to squeeze between two other vans blocked the entire road—it was so tight that in order to inch through, all three vans had to fold in their side mirrors. We stood and waited—Nicky, me, and the postcard guy—in that order. As soon as the van squeezed through, Nicky moved out into the clear, and I quickly scurried up to him in order to get away from the postcard guy. I had a—"I'm-not-safe feeling"—and I wanted to get as much distance between him and me as possible.

It was just a second after that, I reached for my small red camera I had just returned to my pocket moments before. It was gone! Every pocket was completely empty, and the horrible reality that I had just been picked by a pickpocket made its way into my consciousness! My eyes quickly scoured the crowd; I knew it was the postcard guy, but now he was nowhere to be found!

Disbelief, shock, and a total sense of helplessness enveloped me. Nicky and I looked at each other—without words, we knew the hopeless state we were in. Our only recourse was to cry out to the Lord for help, but as I looked around at the sea of people and marketplace busyness, the hopelessness became even more exaggerated......and despairing. Where do you even start to look?

The thief was long gone. I got blank stares in return when I asked a nearby stall worker if he'd seen the guy that just stole my camera—he knew, but the indifference in his eyes, the shrug of the shoulders and deafening silence indicated he was not about to divulge any helpful information to this outsider tourist. We needed a miracle, and the Lord's intervention was our ONLY hope.

For the next few moments, we roamed the market street somewhat aimlessly, all the while praying intensely. My eyes and brain went into search mode like never before, but the more I looked, the more I saw there were an infinite number of places to hide a small red camera. The search was overwhelming and seemed futile. Nicky suggested we go down the street and turn the corner where the market continued. As we headed in that direction, I was fully aware that the moments were passing and wondered if my steps were fruitless. We kept walking slowing while we searched faces, corners of carts, and crevices. "Lord, this is becoming more impossible with each passing minute; we're asking for a miracle. Help us find the camera."

We turned the corner. More stalls. More people. Less hope.

In a hubbub of activity, we walked between more fruit stands, more clothes stands, more toy stands. Then an unexpected event happened. Yes, even after our earnest prayers—an unexpected event.

On my left side, I noticed two men standing under a canopied stall, huddled together and intensely focused. I was drawn in, and then I saw bright RED! My camera!! The man on the right was opening the compartment taking out the SD card that in the next instant was resting in the palm of his hand. I yelled, "Nicky, MY CAMERA!" as I grabbed it and the SD card out of the man's hands. "THAT'S MY CAMERA; YOU STOLE MY CAMERA!!" I screamed! I now had it in my possession, and Nicky was on his way over (since I yelled loudly enough for the whole world to hear!).

I was a broken record as I repeatedly shouted, "THIS IS MY CAMERA; YOU STOLE MY CAMERA!" To my surprise, the man I yanked the camera from put up both his hands as he walked toward me and retorted, "I didn't steal it, honest!" At the same time, thinking the man might come after me and grab the camera and SD card back, Nicky took hold of the man's elbow to let him know he was not just dealing with a half-crazed woman. Then the man started yelling at Nicky, "You owe me 200 shekels!"

Everything happened so fast, and I can't tell you how many times at the top of my lungs I yelled, "THIS IS MY CAMERA; YOU STOLE MY CAMERA!" but as we walked away (and to our amazement, they didn't come after us), my raised voice turned to LOUD PRAISES to Jesus for hearing the cry of our hearts and answering our plea for a miracle.

It was hard for us to believe what had just happened in that last ten to fifteen minutes, but it was true—amid the masses of people and flurry of activity, the Lord so directed our steps to the exact stall, to the exact hands that were holding my little red camera at the exact moment when the SD card was being removed before it got tossed or wiped clean.............safely into my hands!

We stood amazed—how grateful and humbled we were that God so intervened to return even a camera to one careless tourist.

<<>>

"In my desperation I prayed, and the LORD listened; he saved me from all my troubles." —Psalm 34:6 (NLT)

Chapter 8
5 Hp Outboard Witness

<<>>

My very tall, barrel-chested, Army Ranger, paratrooper instructor, cage-fighter, grappling champion friend and I were walking down a long pier heading for my sailboat. You could describe him as a man's man with a great sense of humor and some dark issues buried inside. He loved to fish and the plan was I would sail while he trolled for Saugeye—a cross between a Walleye and a Sauger. His plan was to fish; my plan was to see if the Lord would open him up to talk about some deep spiritual issues that were troubling him.

As we approached my old (bless her heart) 1980 O'Day 22 sailboat, I jokingly said, "As long as the motor starts, we'll go sailing!" Stepping down into the cockpit, I glanced down to look at my old reliable 5 Hp long-shaft outboard motor and . . . it was gone! I always kept it chained to the boat with a hefty anchor chain and lock. I'd been locking it that way for over five years. By then, my friend caught up with me seeing the missing outboard motor, and I said, "Well, my wife and I have given the boat to the Lord, so for some reason, He allowed this to happen."

To get to the open water, one has to motor a quarter of a mile through a narrow channel. My "man's man" friend seriously said that he could make a rope harness, and I could tie the boat to him and he would swim it out to open water! I appreciated the offer, and I'm sure he could have done it, but the prevailing winds typically blew through the channel in the direction of the open water. I told him we would probably make it out, but the wind would be too much for him to swim the boat back. Besides, if something happened to him, I didn't want to go to the trouble of having to winch the big fella out of the water with my mainsheet halyard!

I suggested we go to the other side of the lake where there were some picnic tables and the entrance to a river where he could fish. Before leaving, I called the park police and reported the stolen motor and then grabbed my grill that hung off the stern railing. We drove to the other side of the lake. While he fished, I piled some rocks on the picnic table by the river to hold my grill up since it didn't have legs, and grilled chicken, potato patties, and worked on a salad. We had spent time together before and I knew he was a big eater, so I came prepared. When I called him over to eat, his Styrofoam plate was piled so high with food that the edges were cracking! You should have seen him smile!!

While eating, he started talking. At first, it was general fishing talk, complaining that he didn't even get a bite. Then he got on to how bad he felt for me that my outboard motor had been stolen. I assured him it was in the Lord's hands, and I wasn't worried about it at all! At that point he grew more quiet and started talking about personal things. When he said, "You know, I've never told anybody this before . . . ," I knew then the Lord was at work, and he opened his heart up and we talked and prayed about his issues.

I wondered later how different things might have been if I had gotten mad and angry over the stolen motor. My joy is in the Lord, and not in my stuff. Praise the Lord that the enemy didn't steal away this precious time with my friend. Amen? Amen!!

Postscript: With all three daughters in college, I wasn't able to put much money aside for a new motor. I did manage to save about half of what I needed by the end of the fall when it came time to pull the boat out of the water. I was praying about this because I needed a motor to get my boat to the launch. One day during this time, I was over at my father's house, and out of the blue, he reminded me of something that had happened fifteen years before. I had forgotten all about it! He said, "It was my fault, and it's been bothering me for a long time, so I'll give you the rest of the money you need for your motor." And he did! PTL—now I have a nice new outboard motor!

<<>>

"Now may the Lord of peace himself give you peace at all times and in every way." —2 Thessalonians 3:16 NIV

Chapter 9
Little Boat, Big Boat, Big FREE Boat!

1

<<>>

Sitting in front of my computer, I was cruising through news sites when out of nowhere, I was suddenly overcome with an overwhelming seat-jarring desire to get a sailboat! This was very odd because I'd never had a sailboat, I didn't know how to sail, and I'd never even been sailing. My wife was in the same boat. (Yes, the pun was intended.) Sailing was one of those things we had on the backburner of our minds as something nice to try in the future, but it was in the very far distant future . . . not NOW. Especially "not now" with three kids in college!! Being a rather portly fellow, I could understand a sudden compelling

1. http://www.faithstoriesonline.com/wp-content/uploads/2010/04/Logo-Pics.jpeg

desire to get a milkshake or buy some new cooking tool, but not a sailboat!

Simply out of curiosity, I went to a search engine and typed in "used sailboats," and it returned over a million web pages. (This was in the days before search engines were able to return search pages relative to your location.) I opened the first page and my screen filled with about fifty thumbnail pictures of used sailboats from all over the world. I started clicking on the pics to enlarge them to see what the boats looked like. Towards the bottom of the page, a boat caught my eye. On enlarging the pic, I thought to myself, "Now that's a cool looking twenty-two-foot sailboat. Oddly, that building behind the boat and part of the street looks really familiar. Holy Cow, that's in Vermilion, Ohio, by Lake Erie; I've driven by that building a bunch of times!!" Sitting back in my chair somewhat stunned and baffled all at the same time, I knew that was the boat I was supposed to pursue.

In two weeks we would be attending a Labor Day family reunion at a little church campground called Beulah Beach located on the shore of Lake Erie. The boat was located in Vermilion, Ohio, a small quaint old fishing village just twenty minutes away! I called the boat dealer and found out the boat had not been purchased and was still for sale. I spent the next two weeks reading up on the ins and outs of buying a used sailboat. The next day after the reunion, my wife and I drove into Vermilion to look at the boat. We pulled in the lot where the boat was sitting, and I marveled seeing the building and part of the road that had jumped out at me in the picture on my computer two weeks before.

I started climbing around looking the boat over when the salesman from the dealership across the road walked up. He was a pleasant guy, and he answered my questions about the boat and provided additional information. He gave us the asking price. My wife and I looked at each other, so I verbalized what we were both thinking at the moment. I said to the salesman, "To be honest with you, this is crazy that we are even looking at a boat. We don't even really know why we're here or what we're even thinking . . . since we actually have three kids in college!" He was a really good salesman; he looked us both in the eye and said, "If you have three kids in college, then you NEED a sailboat!" We laughed, offered him a reduced price from what he'd quoted us, whereupon he went across the street to his office to check and shortly returned with an "accepted" response; we shook hands and realized that we had just bought ourselves a boat! Oh boy!

"By the way," he said, "I see the owner of the boat is coming up the hill across the street if you'd like to meet him." We walked across the street and met this friendly Swedish gentleman. My wife and I went in to the boat dealership, signed the paperwork, came out and the former owner of the boat was waiting for us. "Would you to like for me to show you some things about the boat?" he asked. I said, "Sure," but before heading back over to the sailboat, we decided to walk to a shop for some lunch; he graciously bought us sub sandwiches and we walked down to the water's edge by a small museum lighthouse and sat on some rocks. It was a beautiful day with clear blue skies and the sound of waves churning up on the sand with the cries of seagulls floating in the wind overhead.

He took a bite of his sub and asked, "So, how long have you folks been sailing?" My wife and I looked at each other and looked at him and smiled. He looked puzzled and said, "Do you know how to sail?" We slowly shook our heads "no." With astonishment, he said while kind of squinting at us, "Have you EVER been sailing?" "Uh, Noooooo," I said. He burst out laughing, "So you just bought my sailboat, and you not only don't know how to sail, but you've never even been sailing!?!" "Yep," I said with a grin. He looked at both of us, shaking his head and with a smile asked, "Ok, well would you like to go sailing right now?"

We walked over to his house—he had one of the nice houses along the Vermilion River that poured out into Lake Erie. In his backyard was a dock with a twenty-seven-foot sailboat. We got in, he motored out to the river, and on out into Lake Erie. My wife and I were still working on our subs and pop as we sailed for the next two hours. By the time we got back on land, my wife and I were hooked on sailing! We will always be grateful to that fine Swedish man for that sail. We took our new-used boat to Indian Lake for the winter, and the next spring I took yachting lessons and got to crew with the trainers during races. It was awesome! I was so excited after the yachting course to take my boat sailing that I took my wife up to Indian Lake the next weekend. The wind was blowing hard, and there were even whitecaps on Indian Lake, which was rare. As I readied the boat, my wife said into the wind, "Do you notice there are no other boats on the lake??" I retorted, "Good, that's less boats for me to accidentally hit!"

It was so windy I could only use my main sail. As the wind picked up even more, I had to reef my sail (make it smaller) to keep my mast from being ripped from my little boat! I was loving it! I was laughing with delight as we flew across the waves while my wife was screaming with terror!! Years later I met a Norwegian who had sailed his wife and daughter from the North Pole to the South Pole. Seeking some sage advice on sailing, I asked him what advice he would give to a new sailor like myself. Expecting to hear something about wind or navigation he said, "The most important rule is—don't scare your wife!" "Gee, I already broke that one!" I said. We both laughed.

The idea of the sailing ministry started when we noticed the Lord bringing people into our lives with spiritual problems that wanted to go sailing. After the sails were up and we cut the noisy motor, the sound of the wind in the sails and the gurgle of water as we glided across the lake created an atmosphere conducive to folks opening up to talk about their spiritual problems. Or, because of sailing with us, folks often felt closer to us and would open up later to talk about their problems. Either way, we would share with them how God can solve their problems and then have the opportunity and honor to pray with them. In between those 'ministry sails' we would take out friends and family. We even had a blind guy that learned to sail! But that's a story for another time. All in all, boats will come and go, but these spiritual issues are eternal and really do matter to God. After all, didn't Jesus set a great precedent for us . . . it seems to me He tended to hang around the water and boats a good bit!

During those five years of sailing, I kept thinking we needed a logo for our ministry and future website. One day I stopped in a public restroom and entered a stall. Sitting down, I noticed a neatly folded piece of toilet paper laying on a small shelf just above the toilet paper rolls. Someone had made a rough sketch of Jesus hanging on the cross with a boat pilot wheel and anchor in the background and, strangely, had left it in this stall! The message jumped out at me: Jesus is our Savior, our Pilot, and our Anchor in the storms of life. An artist friend of mine named Don made a great logo from those elements—only the cross is empty because Jesus has risen!

On our little boat, we could only sleep four cramped people, and I started thinking about getting a bigger boat. Big to me was a thirty-foot boat that could sleep six, and then we could take folks out for overnight sails. Having spent a lot of time on Lake Erie growing up and attending Ohio State University's Stone Laboratory located on Gibraltar Island in the Bass Islands, I really wanted to sail on Lake Erie. However, the other part of me was thinking, "This is a really dumb idea!" We could barely afford the little boat; how on earth could we ever afford a boat five or ten times what we paid!

One day while visiting Beulah Beach, my wife and I headed over to look at the Sandusky Harbor Marina. As we walk out the dock, I'm looking at all these beautiful sailboats and feel like I'm shopping! I said to myself, "This is crazy! We can't afford a big boat!" I didn't notice it at first because of all the other sailboats, but as we got closer to the end of the dock, I saw a sixty-five-foot double-masted schooner! It was so big, it was moored at the end of the dock! Being a sailboat fan, I was wowed! Then we noticed a wood box with brochures about the boat. As I started reading, I got so excited, I almost fell off the dock! This boat belonged to a sailing ministry!!

The boat was called "The Journey" and was part of B-About Sailing Ministry. They would take troubled kids out sailing and walk them through a program on boat safety, confidence building, and most importantly, share with them about the Love of Jesus! The next week I called the ministry, and we were invited to their next meeting at the marina. B-About Ministry is part of the Christian Boater's Association (CBA), which is a larger body of folks who are Christians and love boating. We met about eight folks, and they were awesome friendly folk! What I was most impressed about was we hardly talked about boats—the focus was on Jesus!!

I told one of the leaders that I was looking for a used thirty-foot boat and had been praying about it for some time. Not long after, I received a forwarded email from the leader from a fellow in Texas. This man and his wife had had a sailing ministry, but sadly due to arthritis and cancer, they could no longer sail. The email said they wanted to give their boat to someone, but only if they would use it in a sailing ministry. They had a Cal29, a twenty-nine foot, eight-inch boat with a new diesel engine that would sleep six! That was close enough to thirty feet for me! I emailed him back, told him about our ministry; he replied and said, "The boat is yours!" What? . . . Really? A FREE big boat! No Way! . . . Only God!

Little boat—Big boat—Big FREE Boat—and a HUGE Praise the Lord!!!

~~ The End ~~

Photo Attributions:

Karen DeM.

Personal photos

Pixabay.com

Jesus Note: If you want to have a relationship with Jesus, then here's how—

"If you want this light and love in your life, say a prayer like this—whether for the first time or to express again your passionate desire to follow Jesus:

Jesus, you are the light of the world. I want to follow you, passionately and wholeheartedly. But my sins have separated me from you. Thank you for your love for me. Thank you for paying the price for my sins, and I trust your finished work on the cross for my rescue.

I turn away from the thoughts and deeds that have separated me from you. Forgive me and awaken me to love you with all my heart, mind, soul, and strength. I believe God raised you from the dead, and I want that new life to flow through me each day and for eternity.

God, I give you my life. Now fill me with your Spirit so that my life will honor you and I can fulfill your purpose for me. Amen.

You can be assured that what Jesus said about those who choose to follow him is true: "If you embrace my message and believe in the One who sent me, you will never face condemnation, for in me, you have already passed from the realm of death into the realm of eternal life!" (John 5:24).

But there's more! Not only are you declared "not guilty" by God because of Jesus, you are also considered his most intimate friend (John 15:15). As you grow in your relationship with Jesus, continue to read the Bible, communicate with God through prayer, spend time with others who follow Jesus, and live out your faith daily and passionately. God bless you!"

Quote taken from the The Passion Translation

https://www.thepassiontranslation.com/

If you prayed the above prayer, I suggest you start reading the Gospel of John.

I prayed this type of prayer on February 2, 1971, and Jesus changed my life—forever!!

Blessings!

Nick Nichols

Don't miss out!

Visit the website below and you can sign up to receive emails whenever Nick Nichols publishes a new book. There's no charge and no obligation.

https://books2read.com/r/B-A-NVTG-FCXVB

BOOKS 2 READ

Connecting independent readers to independent writers.

About the Author

During my 30-year career, I was a water quality chemist, environmental scientist, consultant, and technical writer. In my spare time, I worked on projects in aquaculture, hydroponics, aquaponics, bioremediation, and renewable energy. In addition, I have also been an adjunct instructor at two colleges teaching Cellular Biology and Business Math.

Now I am retired and writing this from an island in South East Asia where I live. My lovely wife has been with me for forty-eight years and we have four awesome adult children and three lovely children in Heaven.

--Nick Nichols

<<>>

Read more at https://authornick.com/.